RICHES

Haiku and Senryu

Richard Picciuto

authorHOUSE®

AuthorHouse™
1663 Liberty Drive
Bloomington, IN 47403
www.authorhouse.com
Phone: 1-800-839-8640

First published by AuthorHouse   7/14/2010

ISBN: 978-1-4520-3334-1 (sc)

Printed in the United States of America
Bloomington, Indiana

This book is printed on acid-free paper.

For Amanda, Justin, Kylee, and Anthony

How far you go in life depends on your being tender with the young, compassionate with the aged, sympathetic with the striving and tolerant of the weak and strong. Because someday in your life you will have been all of these.

George Washington Carver

Foreword

Most poetry has an oral tradition but unlike other poetic forms, haiku and senryu have an element of silence about them... almost a wordlessness, with roots in Buddhist culture. Writers of these two forms seem to live with a more intense awareness of existence, creating these seventeen syllable vignettes on an elevated level of human consciousness. The reader will find the prevailing themes of the transience of life, love and parting, the beauty of nature, mirth and exuberance, as well as wry observations of human nature with its shortcomings and failings. Though the subject matter may be as simple as a birdsong or a moon partly covered by a cloud, the poems are anything but simple. The reader should pause, ingest the scene and reflect upon the associations and echoes implicit in the words.

The Japanese symbols for haiku and senryu were used by the artist as illustrations on the front cover.

The goal of life is to make your heartbeat match the beat of the universe, to match your nature with Nature.

\- Joseph Campbell

Photograph albums
Of people I've never seen
Grandparent's attic

One eye on the clock
Sweating over math exam
Wishing he'd studied

While saying I do
The mother knows her daughter
Is losing freedom

When eyes say one thing
And the tongue says something else
Believe in the eyes

Sometimes with you and
Sometimes against you, currents
In the marriage bed

Playmate of the wind
Cardinal feather drifting
In aimless circles

Furrows in tree bark
Attract downy woodpeckers
Probing for insects

Snowflake on snowflake
View the grandeur of a storm
Slowly evolving

2

Pansies, all colors
Have distinct faces unlike
All other flowers

Swelling streams cascade
Down the rugged mountainside
During the spring thaw

Assassins kill once
Slanderers kill many times
With less punishment

War-torn Slavic town
Still many hungry victims
Throw crumbs to the birds

Taking her candle
She lights her daughter's candle
Still hers remains bright

Turbulent or calm
No hint of finality
Waves in the ocean

Deathbed confessions
Some a final catharsis
Some just one last lie

Flowers by gravestones
Meant for the departed are
More for the mourners

Late night on the road
Light from a bedroom window
Why at three a.m.

Choices for pigeons
Wall Street or Washington Square
Brothels or churches

Like the continents
Slowly drifting apart, the
Couple separates

The puppy races
Towards the yellow school bus
The children are home

Tuesday, six o'clock
Bolstered by shots at the bar
Heading home to wife

An abandoned rake
Stands as a memorial
To the dying farm

The postman carries
A host of sealed emotions
Inside his mailbag

The rust of a year
Is transferred from the snowplow
To the snow crystals

Still feeling depressed
After losing twenty pounds
High school reunion

Leading her shadow
The young woman turns and now
Follows her shadow

Artists with easels
Are as fabled as the barns
On their canvases

He sips fine wine while
Reading Homer's Iliad
Both warm and delight

June sunset's red wine
Has been drunk by the ocean
In silent swallows

September starlight
Enters my windows shining
Silent in my eyes

Preconceived notions
Then she heard two house painters
Speaking of Nietzsche

Error by shortstop
Some parents groan, others cheer
The Little League game

Growing older, her
Appearance declines, yet her
Beauty increases

The chess tournament
A quiet intensity
Advantage for white

As fireworks excite
A veteran sits at home
Jack Daniels in hand

Spring's moss-covered wall
Beckoning children after
Their winter retreat

On Valentine's Day
She gets a rose with no card
Smiling, wondering

The army barracks
He lies on an upper bunk
Reading wife's letter

Working side by side
Unaware of each other
Artist and spider

With eyes averted
Shaking hands with enemies
At the peace table

The spark of music
Ignites a trail in the world
Aiding survival

The sky's mass of clouds
Darken as wind starts to blow
And rain pelts the earth

The bright dragonfly
Darts over the stagnant pond
In a zigzag path

July thunderstorm
Cops direct traffic during
A power outage

Olympic Village
Bringing athletes together
And countries apart

Intimidated
Or else intimidating
The visiting team

As the wind subsides
The lake becomes still again
And mirrors the moon

The front door closes
She breathes a sigh of relief
Children home safely

The moon starts to fade
And romance loses its luster
As the sun rises

Moss on the gravestone
Life clinging to this cold slab
Though not underneath

Stones rubbed by the sands
Slowly washed by the waters
Turning into sand

Late night on the phone
Hearing her voice and the wind
Each speaking to me

Books allow readers
To escape their boundaries
And create frameworks

Waves leaving driftwood
Tracing stories in the sand
Which men decipher

Viewing northern lights
At a farmhouse in Norway
Like flames from a forge

Still alive today
Once eaten by dinosaurs
Ginkgo's fan-shaped leaves

Birds that don't migrate
Extracting seeds from spruce cones
Sustaining themselves

Bells of St. Peter's
Mean nothing to the stray cat
But summon sinners

The relentless surf
Lends a sense of permanence
In its transient worlds

Windy April days
Bend golden forsythia
To the greening grass

On a split rail fence
Red climbing roses lure both
Honeybees and men

The wind drives snowflakes
Past my window to the earth
As crocus bulbs push

Plodding horses' hooves
Keep a cadence while pulling
A sleigh through the woods

Winds whisper in the trees
The world is never silent
Even insects hum

As the storm abates
Tiny crystals blowing hard
Soon become soft flakes

A yellow jacket
Arrives at its colony
With work completed

Sunning on a rock
A snake rests and gains strength for
The search of insects

Single grains of sand
Cast by water and wind form
Great dunes and beaches

Choosing a nanny
While thinking of her mother
Who raised six herself

Autumn work week ends
A stop at the nursery
For daffodil bulbs

Christmas day, age eight
Becoming the engineer
Lionel train set

Passing the cloister
Wondering what called the nuns
To their vocation

The grandfather clock
Never awoke him until
The night that chimes stopped

Where are the clotheslines
Nineteen ninety-nine versus
Nineteen forty-nine

Sun speaking loudly
Calling sleepers to their chores
While the moon whispers

Learning while searching
Not all who wander are lost
Some pursue the arts

The journey is long
From the acorn to the oak
Bucket at the well

White smoke over Rome
Thousands cheer, weep, and give thanks
The keys are transferred

Holding a relic
Made by people of the past
Creating kinship

Petting him gently
The woman speaks to her dog
Her sole companion

The winter solstice
Brings hope for daylight to come
By withholding sun

Distance vanishes
As the fog absorbs the hills
With pearl gray softness

A tiny seed falls
And blue spruces germinate
So falcons can nest

Birds sing ancient songs
And fly the uncharted skies
With awesome grandeur

Writing poetry
In moments of solitude
Helps one know oneself

The darkening sky
Faint crescent moon appearing
Twilight calm descends

One tree is tallest
One animal leads the pack
And so with mankind

Seed to tree to seed
Nature's timeless sequence is
The earth's signature

For seventeen years
The cicada lies dormant
Erupting in song

The gate to nowhere
And the gate to everywhere
Open the same way

He saddened as his
Lover's eyes betrayed her words
And mirrored her heart

Two ticket stubs lay
Hidden in her drawer from
A time she holds dear

Sensing her child's pain
Thinking, silently searching
For words of comfort

Snowman now built, the
Children head to the kitchen
Steaming hot chocolate

Frozen Nazi corpse
On the outskirts of Moscow
Pelted by the sleet

While stirring the pot
In fire she created
She also got burnt

The ice fisherman
At a Minnesota lake
Longs for solitude

The cream out of reach
She cuddles the kitten and
Tells her she trusts her

The chimes strike midnight
The night becoming a cloak
Covering sinners

Sand sculptures at beach
Loved by sculptor and viewer
The tide is rising

The homeless beggar
New York side of the tunnel
With liquor on breath

A tree glazed with ice
Interprets nature's magic
With crystal clearness

Faithful to the past
With an eye to the future
Cree tend to their land

Eyes that see the world
Interpreters of actions
Not their creators

Author in a trance
Able to translate his dreams
For use in his work

Winter night vision
Crescent moon through leafless trees
Hangs next to my bed

Mystical mushrooms
No stone or log can stop them
For their time has come

Mount Vesuvius
Above the bay of Naples
Poised and smoldering

The spray of the wave
Small sandpipers appearing
With welcoming songs

Full moon reflected
By thousands of crystals in
Drifts of white stillness

Boats in the bathtub
The youngster captains the ships
Of his armada

January moon
Lights up the world when it's dark
Nobler than the sun

March wispy white clouds
Bring on wistful emotions
My feelings for her

Faithless sundial
Counting hours in sunlight
While men count them all

Small streams freeze over
Lonely hills sleeping under
Winter starlit skies

Writing a letter
To a friend by candlelight
The flame warms her hands

Lovely, lonely girl
All she can see is her own
Image in his eyes

White chrysanthemum
Heralds lazy autumn's days
And frost's mosaics

As sunlight moves west
Tiger lilies are closing
And shadows move east

The present gets lost
When the future is pulling
And the past pushes

In cemeteries
No one mourns for those who died
Ninety years ago

Confessing his sins
He kneels at the church altar
Asking forgiveness

The hounds sniff the air
Catching the scent of a fox
Followed by hunters

Solitary hawk
On the branch of a dead tree
Scanning the swampland

A vortex of leaves
Crackles with memories of
Childhood street football

The graceful white birch
At the edge of the forest
Yields to brash March winds

Glowing so softly
Seemingly lit from within
The polar bears' fur

Birds nest high in large
Trees that are ever the same
And never the same

Snow on the wood pile
Searching for a cherry log
To anchor the flame

At an old schoolyard
Viewing trees with initials
Now out of our reach

Through strong gusts of wind
The butterfly zigzags, yet
Still lands on the rose

The able woman
Must carry her purse while the
Fair maiden does not

Owls in the forest
Don't bemoan their condition
Nor weep for their sins

The stoic gray wolf
Cannot understand reasons
Why men set their traps

Two children wonder
As the funeral passes
Why car lights are on

The frightened rabbit
Adds wings to his feet while the
Turtle shrinks from sight

At the oceanside
Poets petition the moon
While waves keep crashing

The artist's version
Of the mountain does not speak
Of the climber's plight

Reading at bedtime
Father with children
Teaching each other

One mountain shadows
Another mountain that has
Never seen the sun

Ruins of Pompeii
House of the tragic poet
Buried under ash

August sun captures
The mist of the waterfall
Rising with the roar

Powerful spring gale
Courses through the forest as
Nature prunes her trees

Stones' varied layers
Hold memories of the past
And speak to our souls

The streetlight accents
White snowflakes that touch my face
And coat the hemlock

Walking the mountains
Not seeing boundary lines
Which are on the map

The sun warms her face
Easter Sunday while praying
At her husband's grave

Even with no wind
The flight of the butterfly
Very erratic

The quiet gray sky
Of a November morning
Soon snowflakes will fall

Viewing June sunrise
With your child, is as special
As life ever gets

Harboring secrets
The most silent place on earth
The barren desert

The scent of clover
Brings thoughts of mowing the lawn
Before playing ball

A young boy looks for
The returning oriole
To pick the same tree

A blue jay feeding
Upon the berries of trees
Other jays planted

One living during
The ice age could not know of
Earth's changing climate

A polar bear treads
The vast endless sea of white
Arctic tundra ice

Lives are beginning
As other lives are ending
Balance must be served

Not even locksmiths
Can open the heart that hides
Her secret feelings

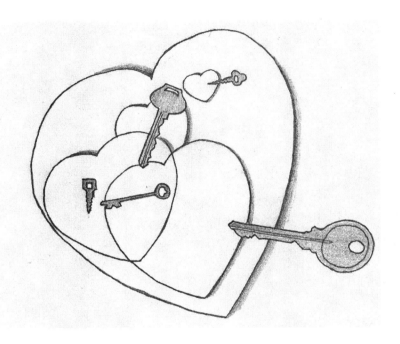

After the leaves fall
Winter's colorless landscapes
Alter mankind's moods

The humble raven
Is revered for its cunning
And resourcefulness

Eagles stay aloft
By riding thermal updrafts
With little effort

During the deep freeze
Polar bears must navigate
Featureless landscapes

Imagination
Cannot surpass the beauty
Of one yellow rose

Sculpted by the wind
Each cloud a whimsical form
Which men cannot chart

Happy or lonely
Some grieving, some rejoicing
Affairs of the heart

Birds drink from the brook
As it winds through the forest
On its odyssey

Searching the elm's side
The woodpecker plays his tune
On the rotting wood

Michelangelo
Philosopher with chisel
God guides his hammer

The spectrum won't show
The colors seen in her hair
When bathed in sunshine

Forever silent
The moon speaks to all creatures
And sets their compass

At the local pub
Friends embellish March snowfall
Now up to four feet

A timid young girl
Stands close to the teacher while
Other children play

April winds stripping
Blossoms from trees as I peer
Through rain swept windows

We did not speak, yet
The eloquence of silence
Linked us together

Philosophy class
Now I know others have thought
What I also have

Strangers we meet, but
Strangers no more, for we have
Touched by our meeting

Holding an old coin
Wondering what it could tell
About where it's been

His vision of her
Her image of herself is
Some distance apart

On sunken concrete
Puddle reflecting spire
March wind breaks the view

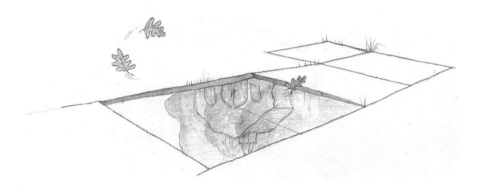

A clear winter night
Wanting to drink hot coffee
From the big dipper

The falling of leaves
Disclose the secrets that birds
Held through the summer

Gazing into her
Pale blue eyes remembering
His sister's first doll

Primitive men had
More reverence for rainbows
Than men of today

After the sun sets...
One by one the stars emerge
And night creatures stir

Birds fluff their feathers
Facing brisk March winds as the
Days become longer

Growing in clusters
Birches sway together with
Strength in unity

The phlox in the field
Survive because of others
That met life's challenge

Humid August day
Two hundred degree asphalt
Wilts the paving crew

The military
Once the order is given
Bombs can't go upward

First breath of morning
Suddenly evening arrives
Life is a whisper

She writes long letters
Because she doesn't have time
To compose short ones

Somewhere in lake's depths
As fishermen bait their hooks
The trout search for food

Seeds hold promises
Of a thousand forests that
Will shelter the birds

Delivering mail
In July or December
People talk weather

Psychiatric ward
Visitors anxious as they
Engage relatives

Mumps epidemic
The boy sits on front porch with
Quarantine arm band

Whirling and splashing
A crimson cloud of blood drifts
The predator strikes

Wolves convey their moods
To the other pack members
By body language

The mountain lion's
Easygoing behavior
Belies its intent

Bears wait patiently
As the salmon nears until
Striking instantly

Sweatshirts in July
Short sleeves for Thanksgiving show
Quirks of the weather

An August hailstorm
The black pavement becomes white
Men wonder, cows graze

Mirrors sometimes lie
Telling trifles and needing
Interpretation

Weeds in a garden
The same as children pick to
Bring to their mothers

Finding a pine cone
From deep beneath a snowdrift
The chipmunk survives

Double rainbow arcs
Blaze above the spruce forest
In the arctic spring

Summer night descends
Vibrant with the hum of life
Owls' vigils start

The coming of spring
Robins and forsythias
Are its harbingers

Authors poised with pens
Think eternal themes slanted
By experience

Her dreams forgotten
She sweeps the ashes of sleep
Like sand from her eyes

An empty playground
Falls prey to diving bats while
Awaiting the dawn

The unruffled owl
Patiently watches the mouse
Leave his snowbound nest

Birds in the graveyard
Have no notion of the dead
While feasting on worms

Huckleberry Finn
His used copy is dog-eared
With notes in margins

Apples reddening
In the early autumn chill
Bees become sluggish

The house facing south
Has no snow on its front roof
And a white rear roof

A gray messenger
Is noted by the mirror
In her auburn hair

From across the room
The fluttering lashes speak
To her friend's husband

The loudest rebuke
The youngster ever heard was
His parent's silence

A true artist is
Set aside from the masses
Due to his insight

Shadowy stark dreams
Instructing their creators
With nightly visits

Last winds of winter
Fade into an echo as
Spring patterns evolve

Blue jays and finches
Fly different airways and
Seek different foods

The new-fallen snow
Sparkling with reflected light
From stars reaching down

Hawthorns and dogwoods
Each beautiful, yet unique
Neither is better

Concentric circles
Widen from a quiet pond
Jumping frog splashes

When his door closes
The monster under his bed
Looms large in his mind

Gray of November
Cannot dampen the spirit
Of migrating birds

Damp day at graveyard
Slowly reading epitaphs
Too many youngsters

In the pumpkin field
Looking from orange to blue
Watching hawks circle

Soldiers on parade
Never looking left or right
Capturing crowd's heart

In the rock garden
The chipmunk comes from nowhere
With escape routes planned

One student cramming
On the night before exams
While her roommate sleeps

Morning sun captures
The radiance of dewdrops
On the spider web

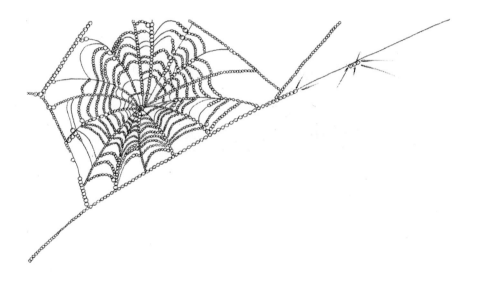

Like a gray teapot
The squirrel holds an acorn
Unmoved by the wren

Spirited black cat
Licks her young in bitter March
Unafraid of fate

The nun on retreat
Holds the cherry blossom close
A tear on her cheek

Hoeing his garden
An old man straightens up while
Refilling his pipe

November reminds
The moon is a stark mistress
Yet I adore her

Summer dusk descends
Scanning heavens for Venus
The bright evening star

He left this morning
Her mind thinks of nothing else
What of the children

A beautiful day
If all flowers bloom at once
But a dull future

A cloud blocks the sun
The air suddenly cooler
He grabs a sweatshirt

Their unspoken rule
Flirting allowed as long as
It remains just that

Wanting fresh powder
He skis the edge of the trail
Steep, yet less traveled

The sunset attacks
Maine's sugar maples that are
Accented yellow

A bolt of lightning
The quaking aspen shatters
Hawks relocate nests

Close to the streetlight
The hemlock casts its shadow
Purple on the snow

All life has order
Jays leave and return each year
The sun sets each day

Last rays of sunlight
Turning clouds into palettes
Of purples and reds

What are his motives
To be admired or loved
By the girl he courts

The renegade fox
Is dancing to the music
His forebears composed

Poet penning thoughts
That will outlive him and still
Give light to others

Long arctic winters
Keep villagers cabin-bound
Around their warm stoves

Dead tree on the knoll
Seems to suggest a power
After life has gone

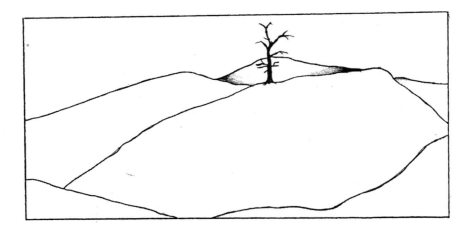

Colonies persist
Plants tend to cluster as do
Birds of a feather

Cold air replaces
Warm air rising to great heights
Causing the thunder

December snowfall
Creates silence in the woods
And softens wind chimes

Midnight Christmas mass
With faint candles flickering
Prompting reflection

The edge of the woods
August blackberry bushes
Feed hungry blackbirds

Spring pansies arrive
With their variant colors
And lovely faces

By staying asleep
Some secrets that the dawn holds
Will never be heard

Fascinating from
A different perspective
Sundial in shade

Visit to psychic
She predicts he will travel
As all of us do

A full autumn moon
Skittish Boston terrier
Gentle strokes calm him

Spring moon over Rome
The same moment in Paris
Two poets create

Restless flocks swarm high
Over the leafless forest
Sensing their mission

Facts limit the mind
Concepts lead to greater thoughts
And brighter visions

Merely stepping stones
Mankind's former achievements
Challenge men anew

Time is impartial
One can develop wisdom
At many ages

Game in the balance
While standing at the foul line
He inhales deeply

A calm autumn day
Oak's vivid scarlet leaves float
Free in the forest

The lead changes hands
In the formation of geese
And will change again

While birds are in flight
The smaller pecks the larger
That is less agile

Strolling hand in hand
Lovers searching for sea glass
On a Cape Cod beach

Man sitting on bench
With thoughts and remembrances
Of his third grade crush

Peering through my eyes
She notices wheels turning
People read people

On cold winter nights
Men blow on their hands for warmth
With fog from their mouths

A gnarled, stunted pine
Living amongst mountain rocks
Despite shallow roots

Dog days of August
Even flowers are listless
Longing for showers

Finch on the feeder
Feathers are strewn underneath
Predators lurking

Alaskan sled dogs
Become a vital resource
For winter travel

July lightning bugs
About to be captured by
Boys carrying jars

Decades have passed since
I was nine, yet she still roams
The edge of my mind

Ducks swim even when
Ice at the edge of the pond
Signals December

Volcanoes erupt
Rivers of molten lava
Paint the earth anew

Men name the planets
And chart their courses but can
Never direct them

The locking of horns
A dominance of the herd
The imperative

The purple-leafed plum
With such delicate blossoms
That last just one week

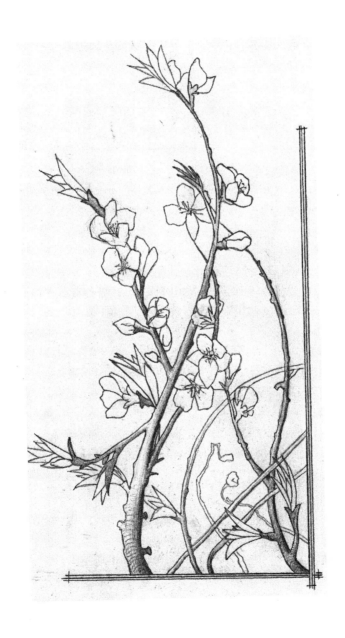

Cloudless May morning
The cat lies on the carpet
Where she finds the sun

The master sculptor
Extracts night, day, dusk, and dawn
From the marble slabs

Without any names
Stars would still shine and roses
Have petals and thorns

Hushed predawn darkness
With horizon full of stars
The birds will sing soon

When the wind subsides
And the storm spends its fury
Wolves return to hunt

Standing on the beach
The rhythm of the ocean
Whispering, roaring

Christmas Eve at home
The best loved day of the year
Cookies for Santa

Once whittled by knives
The flute that plays her music
And her daughter's doll

Like a lightning bolt
The osprey dives with talons
Striking a salmon

Not to be outdone
Mosquitoes will also eat
At July picnics

Snowy pine needles
Quiver as the chickadee
Flits from branch to branch

The pond reflects reeds
And cattails in wavy lines
Yielding to May breeze

Overcome with sleep
The old dog naps on the floor
At his master's feet

Housebound in snowstorm
Glad I have wine, bread, and cheese
Some books and dry wood

After the first frost
Apples in orchard ripen
Enough for picking

My shadow lengthens
As I cut my Christmas tree
Gone now its shadow

After the sun sets
Night is a place I visit
To discover light

Overcome with fear
Hand frozen on the doorknob
Turn or pull away

Vanity of man
Instead of Afterglow Lanes
We have Marla Drives

Summer browning grass
After September rainfall
Becomes green again

Highway accident
The rubbernecker goes home
Telling of horrors

An arctic snowstorm
Blinding at the horizon
Induces stupor

Winter in Oslo
An old man leaning on cane
Watching children sled

Bending birches gleam
As ice glazes their branches
Mindset of winter

Vatican City
Christianity's center
All roads lead to Rome

About the Author

Richard Picciuto

Richard majored in English at the College of St. Elizabeth in Convent Station, New Jersey, where he was introduced to the specialty of writing haiku by Professor Frank J. Korn. Since then, he has expanded his interests into a subset of the haiku form, namely senryu, a more human-styled poetic form.

He lives in Winston-Salem, North Carolina following a business career in his former hometown of Livingston, New Jersey. In addition to poetry, Richard writes short stories and is in the process of drafting a memoir.

About the Artist

Judy Drake

Judy Drake took her first private art lessons at age ten and studied at the Newark, NJ School of Fine Arts. Following this artistic path, she ultimately became a career kitchen and bath designer. She continues to dabble, draw, and design...now turning her talents to interpretive art. Judy is the respected creator of 'Joodles,' petite, complex abstracts that are fanciful and lineal geometric pieces of fun. She lives with her husband in McCall, Idaho, enjoying gardening and contributing to the community.

LaVergne, TN USA
28 July 2010
191162LV00003B/6/P